JN134063

SUPER BOWL
NFL
TO THE
EPIDEMIC

Paris Texas

THOSE THAT
BECOME OBSOLETE
TO THE
EPIDEMIC

THAT
BSOLETE
HE

THOSE THAT
COME OBSOLETE
TO THE

り商店街
EPIDEMIC
Steelers

旅人の宿
平和荘
つぼや焼
古民藝
Paris Texas

THOSE THAT
BECOME OBSOLETE
TO THE
EPIDEMIC

Texas

Mobby's
¥1,000
¥1000
NFL
Steelers
TAMPA BAY

Paris Texas

SEIDO
NSTORE
ティックみらい
新鮮直送 オリオン生ビール 樽生
¥1300
¥1080
THOSE THAT
ECOME OBSOLETE
THE

Paris Texas

Steelers

手すりに登らない
で下さい
T CLIMB FENCE

PHOTO BY *Masaki*

メンバーが使い捨てカメラで撮りおろし！

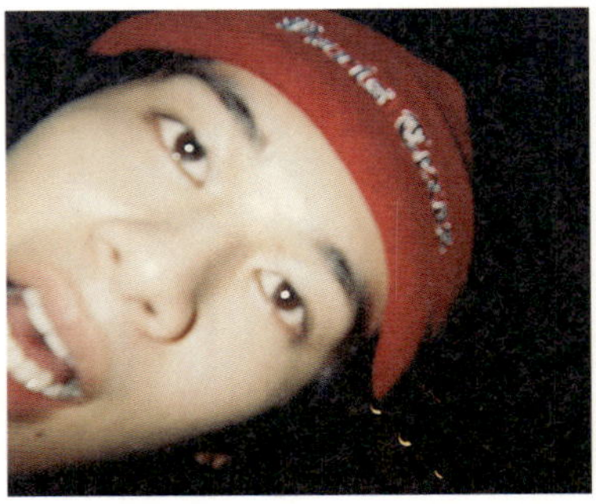

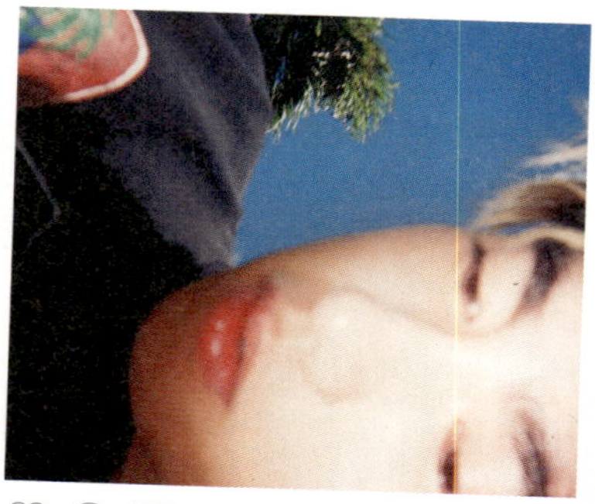

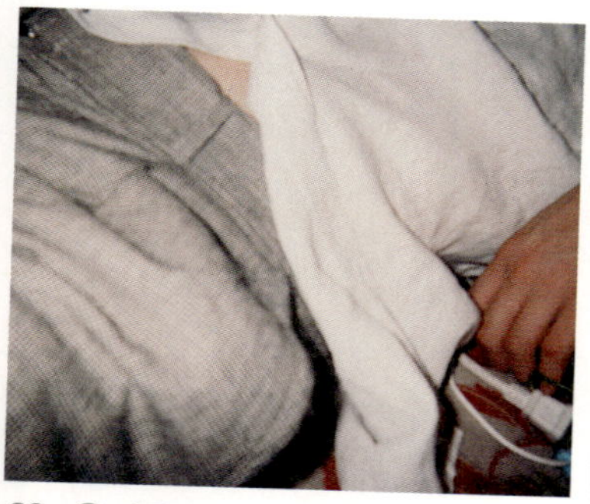

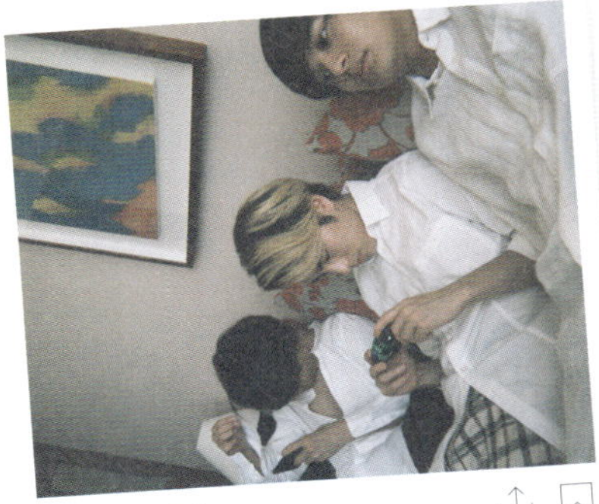

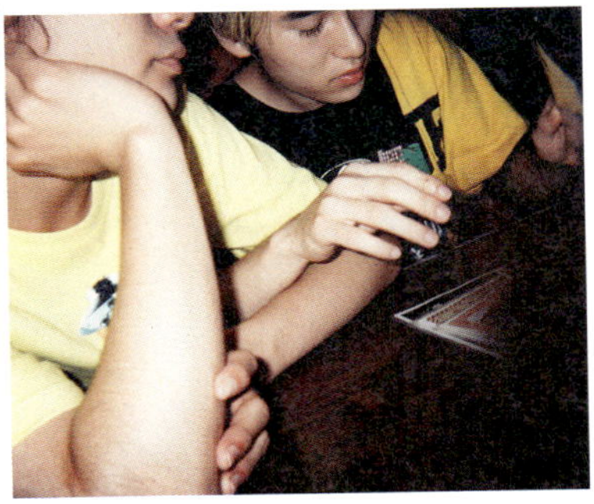

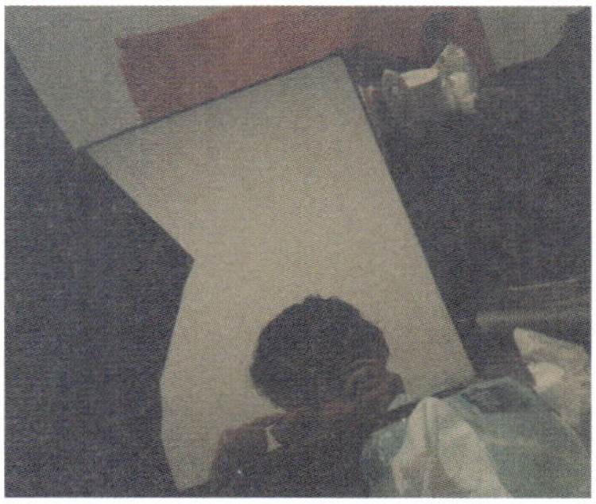

Paris Texas
OBSOLETE TO THE EPIDEMIC

Paris Texas
Evisen skateboards

OSE THAT
BECOME
BSOLETE
TO THE

BLUE SEAL

dairy bar
ice cream and milk
Paris Texas
BLUE SEAL

KANGOL

INTERNATIONAL DAIRIES RYUKYUS LTD
THOSE THAT
BECOME OBSOLETE
TO THE

Paris

大智
DISH//

三大夜景 NAGASAKI

ÆON MALL
イオンモール宮崎
Starting Over
DISH//

DISH// スペシャルイベント
観覧無料

JR九州ホテル長崎
TRANDOR トランドール
長崎銘品蔵
Nagasaki-K-Board

ÆON MALL
イオンモール宮崎

ÆON MALL
イオンモール宮崎
Starting Over
DISH//

DISH

Mall

8D
県道
145
熊本
3丁目

熊本市広域詳図
Starting Over
12th single 2018.7.11 release
DISH//
DISH
インストアイベント決定!
9.22
つばめ
TSUBAME
熊本
Kumamoto
9D

P
IN

PHOTO BY *Takumi*

メンバーが使い捨てカメラで撮りおろし！

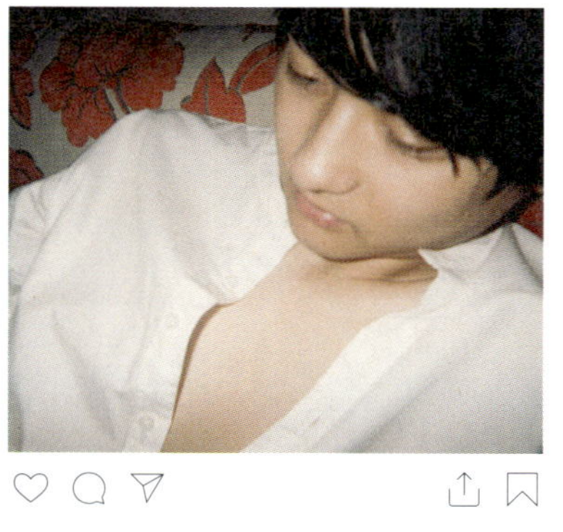

PHOTO BY *To-i*

メンバーが使い捨てカメラで撮りおろし！

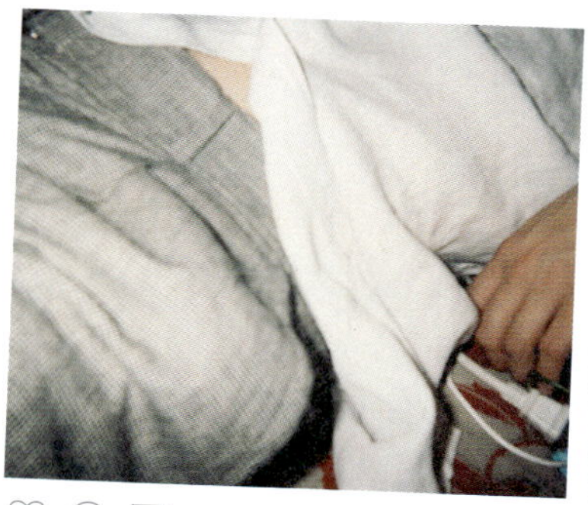

SPORTSSTUFF
GREAT

GREAT BIG MABLE

PHOTO BY *Daichi*

メンバーが使い捨てカメラで撮りおろし！

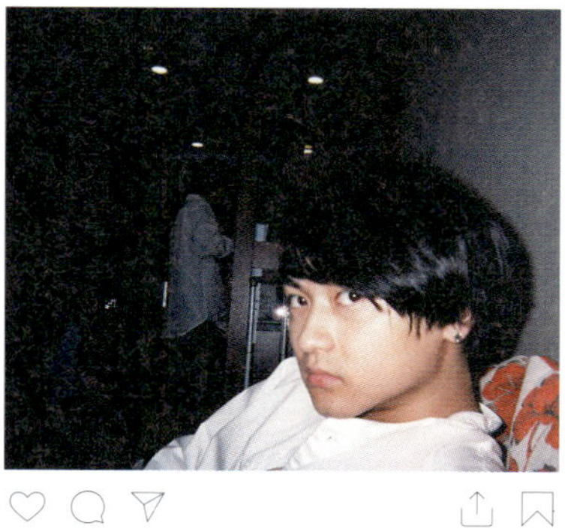

STEAK
88
Japan.
Tax-free
Shop
TAX
FREE
STEAK HOUSE

雪塩ちんすこう
YUKISIO

for 1000yen 3个
どれでも選べる
without tax(税別
全国

宝和商

DRAGON GATE
ドラゴン・キッド
ビセガネ獣
アプレミディ
小書店にて絶賛発売中!!

菓子屋栄町店

ひまわり
ハンバーグの店

DISH//

3rd Photo Book

沖縄定食